# Introduction

How to begin a piece of work is difficult for most of us. Each has to find their own paths.

In this book we explore our separate pathways, challenges and obstacles on the avenue towards a resolved body of work.

Some of these experiences might echo your own thoughts or support and even reassure you when undergoing the crisis of confidence that accompany the creative process in every field. It happens to us all and often a second opinion or fresh pair of eyes helps.

Over the years we have found that working in themes or with a thrust of an idea give structure to our work and it is a philosophy that has proved successful with students.

Textiles is a huge area and full of wonderful diversions so if anything really satisfying is to be achieved then focus is the only way.

Themes afford the opportunity for exploring a range of ideas over a series so that the experience gained in one piece of work can be carried forward to the next and developed further. It encourages us to delve more deeply and work through the obvious before hopefully capturing the essence of a subject.

Most people find that all pieces in a series are not equally successful and sometimes it is possible to overwork a series. It is often best to stop when the next idea is a struggle rather than a passion.

Our basic approach is initially based on observation combined with personal experience of the subject so anecdote and historical perspective play a part.

By working in sequence we build on these experiences and hopefully explore deeper.

We hope that these genuine reflections of our pathways echo your own thoughts and personal experiences.

If you are just starting out then they may give you the confidence to respond positively to some of the setbacks that are bound to occur.

Whether a series will succeed or not is obviously important but a major part of the excitement is the pathway and exploration along the way so we hope you will view these very personal accounts with this much in mind.

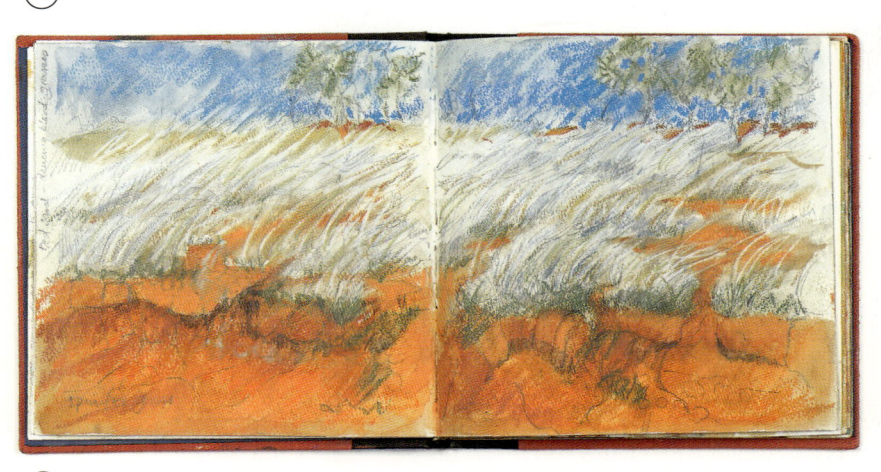

**Inside Front Cover:**
*Detail from 'Fleeting Moment'*
*(see page 5).*
*A range of matt, shiny and metallic machine threads worked on soluble fabric. Inspired by Tunisian seascapes.*

**Right:**
*Sketchbook pages. Aquarelle crayons were used to depict:*
*A) Underwater images in a Tunisian sea.*
*B) Grasses and red soil in Australia.*

2 - DOUBLE VISION

# Selecting a Theme - Jan's Approach

In general my work is based on my observations and memories returning to much loved themes triggered by new experiences and environments.

From my student days until now, light effects on varying surfaces, such as aspects of landscape, have always fascinated me. These observations are often fleeting and invariably difficult to record sufficiently to inform the work thus continually presenting ever-changing challenges.

I enjoy working with a theme, which allows time to explore several avenues of thought. Words and brief descriptions can sum up the atmosphere of a certain place preferably with accompanying sketches. Photographs can be helpful to present factual elements of form but they seldom capture or emphasise those special images that had caught your interest and intrigued you in the first instance. A very quick diagram with descriptive words and colour notes will often contain more useful information along with a genuine emotional response.

In the past I have enjoyed making subtly coloured pieces inspired by Crete, Turkish seascapes, as well as exploiting the strong colourings and lush foliage of New Zealand and strident images experienced in Israel.

Other countries have also afforded intriguing glimpses but time has not been sufficient to digest and explore beneath the superficial initial responses. When embarking on a theme, I try to 'walk before I can run' giving time for the ideas and compilations to grow and expand. Allowing time to understand the basic characteristics and reaching beneath the surface to the soul of the piece has to be a constant goal so enabling you to work on several aspects within the theme. This helps to avoid the desire to include every appealing feature in a single work. One idea will often 'feed' another.

Embarking on a new theme fills me with trepidation. Initially there is always the fear of failure lurking in the back of my mind. The passion or fascination for the subject is constant but that special 'something' may be lost in the work process!

My aim is to create a stitched textile to be viewed in two stages so as to capture an atmospheric image when viewed from a distance as well as revealing other colour, textural qualities, nuances and details on closer inspection.

**Left Page:**
*All the examples shown were worked by machining onto soluble cloth to create a new fabric. Fabric snippets and hand stitches were incorporated a) and c)*

A) *'Rose Evening'.*
   *Crete series 1991 (detail)*
B) *'Forest Texture'.*
   *New Zealand series 1996 (detail)*
C) *'Sövalye Island'.*
   *Turkish series. 1997.(detail)*
D) *'Passages of Time II'.*
   *Israel series.1997 (detail)*

**Above:**
*'First Light' (46cms x 49cms).*
*Scrims, wool tops and various machine threads including Madeira Tanne and Burmilana. This was inspired by a dawn walk in Kings Canyon and the early morning sun suddenly lighting up the sheer wall of the canyon.*

**Left:**
*Sketchbook. Aquarelle crayons and Koh-I-Noor water-based dyes depicting the eroded slabs of stone on the ground.*

# Seascapes

The sea has been a recurring part of my life engendering so many memories. As with other artists working in a variety of media, I have spent many happy hours gazing at is transient colours and moods. It is only in recent years that I have attempted to draw or paint its rhythms and translucent hues which are constantly changing depending on the tides, time of day, seasons and weather patterns. Spending long periods of time observing the movements of the water is mesmerising, almost meditative, and allows you to dream a little and to think through ways to exaggerate certain responses to a given time or memory.

The medium of fabric and thread allow more expressive choices of surface qualities perhaps depicting reflections, a subtle gleam as well as the ability to layer, to see through to the distance or into the mysterious deep.

Reflections are the most difficult and tantalising to capture in a drawing. Just as you think that you have deduced a particular rhythmic pattern, a change of water movement sets up new ones thus effecting the linear imagery, colour and visibility of the seabed below.

The ebb and flow of the water offers another challenge as the movement changes dramatically whether it flows gently over sand or splashes through small pebbles and stones at the water's edge. Rough water disturbs the seabed and colours appear more opaque whereas calmer days allow clearer, translucent views through the water with intriguing distortions.

Changing weather and passing clouds affect the colour bands dramatically as well as the tonal variations where the sky meets the sea. The colour changes so rapidly that mixing the colours on the palette is a race against time. I find this an enjoyable challenge!

Studying life under the water is equally fascinating presenting a wealth of interesting structures. New plant life springing from the debris of the sea-bed. Decaying leaves, surprisingly coloured algae, and other parasites all appear to be arranged in networks and rhythms alongside flowing patterns in the sand. Water movements continually change due to the weather or the tides setting up intriguing and often complex shapes. The ongoing problem is how to capture the essence without being too literal. Drawing these images also proved difficult although a snorkel and a diver's board and pencil helped!

Partnering these observations with emotional responses to a particular time, place or country is confusing and frustrating but at times magical.

Ⓐ   Ⓑ

**Top Left:**
Two sketchbook pages showing attempts to capture the colours of sea and sky in the rapidly fading light.

**Left:**
Two studies of sea worked by layering machine stitches on soluble cloth.
A) 'Late Evening' (16.5cms x 25cms).
B) 'Fading Light' (15cms x 27cms).

**This Page:**
'Fleeting Moment' (80cms x 145cms). This piece which was inspired by some of the colour studies shows many layers of straight and zig-zag stitches. The sky area was worked in matt threads and to contrast, the sea in shiny or metallic threads. Much 'under-painting' in stitch was carried out in the attempt to capture the subtle and elusive colours. Metallic thread was used in the bobbin and played a large part in depicting the glint of the sea without it being too obvious.

# The Red Centre:
## The green was there but it's the red you remember.

My resolve was to create several pieces that captured and celebrated the emotions experienced while travelling through the Red Centre of Australia. I set out to reflect the vast scale of the landscape, the intimate and mystical elements found within the rock formations as well as the sense of history and the knowledge that it has been a special place for millions of years. The wondrous colours, the special light qualities emphasising the intriguing rock surfaces, along with the sheer joy of being there, inspired a number of creative pathways.

The visitor to this area is constantly aware of the lifelines and rhythmic patterns created by wind and water erosion as well as the ancient and sacred places. Your visual and cerebral senses are stretched to the limit and the challenge was to harness and hopefully capture some of these qualities within stitched works. Along with magical colours and textures, all can capture a mood, a memory, or an essence of a time and place.

The first glimpse of the red soil was mind-blowing. Amazing oranges and reds and due to wetter conditions in recent years an unexpected numbers of grasses and shrubs in shades of grey and blue greens. The complementary colours giving sharp contrasts. Although aware of the green, it is the red that lingers in your mind.

The aim throughout has been to keep the pieces very simple and initially understated, reflecting the overwhelming effect of the vibrant colours and the first impressions of the expansiveness of the landscape. As the terrain became more familiar, closer observations exposed ancient and eroded surfaces accompanied by an immense sense of history.

I have attempted to keep the drawing and tonal qualities under control to maintain the simplicity as well as capturing the overall feeling of my initial reactions. Closer inspection of the work may reveal more observational details of form and surface texture.

Kata Tjuta (The Olgas) is made from a conglomerate of gravel, pebbles and boulders cemented

**Above:** 'The Edge of Shade' (41cms x 48cms) inspired by Kata Tjuta (The Olgas). The terrific tonal and colour changes were appealing. In the sun, vibrant oranges and reds glowed whereas similar rock surfaces in the shade appeared the colour of crushed raspberries with hints of blue and purple. Gravel, pebbles and boulders cemented by sand and mud make up this conglomerate. The rounded lumps and bumps within the rock face are very different from the flaky rhythms to be found at Uluru (Ayers Rock).

**Below:** *Sketchbook page showing one of the typical types of landscape to be seen n the Red Centre. Aquarelle and wax crayon.*

in sand and mud. In contrast Uluru (Ayers Rock) is a coarse grained sandstone (arkose) and has a wondrous ridged and flaky appearance as this exposed surface is caused by the rusting of the iron in the arkose. Water erosion over the years has formed steep valleys, hollows, holes and pools.

The colour of both areas was stunning and ranged through blues, slate, greys, purples, deep reds and ochres in the shadows and deep crevices to the amazing overall oranges often seen in the typical tourist photograph of the rocks bathed in sunshine.

Kings Canyon is spectacular especially early in the day. The colours differ from the other sites. Ochres and gingers predominate the maroons, purples and blues with hints of green as plants seem to grow in the tiniest crevice. Horizontal bands and stripes of the rock walls contrasted fabulously with the impressive stepping stones created by the patch worked slabs of stone on the ground.

*'Ancient Ridge' (38cms x 72cms). The bold colour of the soil in the Red Centre was emphasised by the green and almost turquoise rounded shrubs growing on the slopes. Some heavier fabric fragments were incorporated in the lower third of the panel in order for the additional weight to help the 'hang' or fall of the cloth. Curtain 'bead' weights sometimes tend to make the edges curl.*

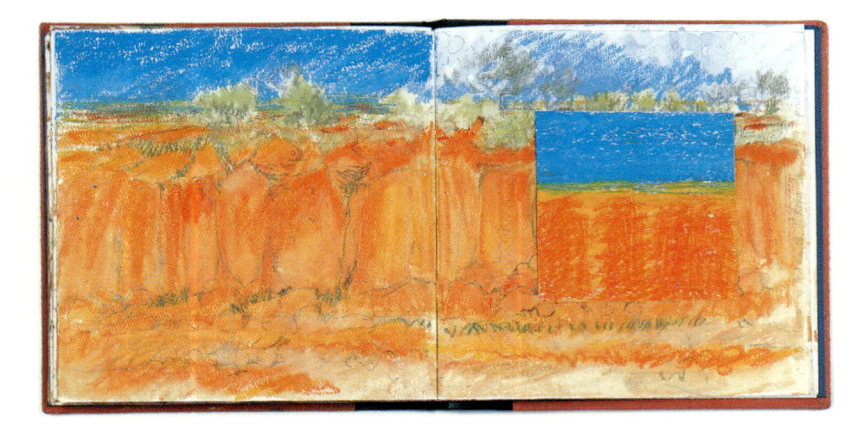

In some pieces the aim is for the viewer to be invited into the picture and to imagine what is beyond a ridge, around a corner or in a hollow.

The immense stature of the rock surfaces as well as the vast sense of space within the whole area was at times surprising, exciting and awesome and offered contrasts to more intimate close ups of secret places.

## Starting

On starting a new body of work, I refer to my observational sketches and notes. I then paint several paper permutations very quickly applying the colour, usually 'Brusho' with a broad brush or sponge applicator. This action sometimes helps me to maintain a simple image, to consider the scale and hopefully capture the essence of the subject.

I sometimes choose to exaggerate one aspect and leave out others if I feel that the composition will become too busy and complicate the main thrust of the piece. Taking myself on a 'mind' walk without looking at any visuals can help to isolate the features that linger and made the biggest impression. A distillation of my feelings and memories are the aspects I then focus on.

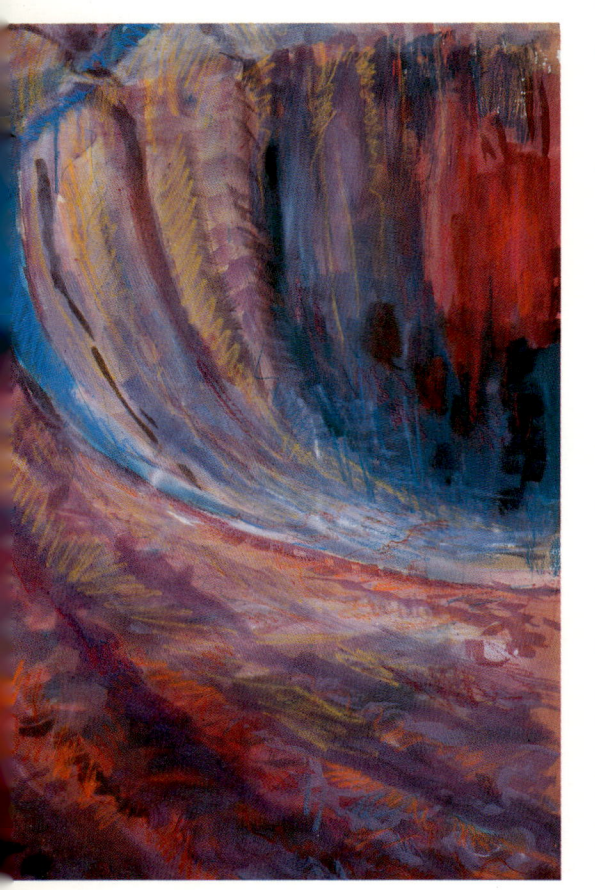

**Top:**
Sketchbook page showing first drawing of the red soil.

**Left:**
Coloured design on lining paper using 'Brusho' paints.

**Right:**
'Searing Heat' (67cms x 64cms). Initially the intention was to capture and harness the amazing impact of the contrasting colours of blue and orange as well as the space. I took a risk with the composition. In general a panel should not have a line dangerously near dividing the piece in half. The aim was for the viewer to feel part of the landscape with the ability to see for miles and miles.

DOUBLE VISION · 9

# Methods & Helpful Tips

Recently I have selected to work on soluble cloth for the following reasons:

- It enables me to 'underpaint' in stitch so that any layers peaking through are integrated.
- Gives a non fraying edge.
- Creates a pleasing and comfortable surface to hand stitch into if appropriate.
- It offers the choice of creating a range of unique textural qualities from gossamer laceworks to chunky dimensional surfaces.
- It enables you to have total control over making the cloth.

All the pieces illustrated have been worked on the heavier 'solusheet'. It sits comfortably in the frame, is non-slippery and does not tear.

To obtain a soft finish it may take several rinses in clean water followed by a short rinse in a fabric conditioner. The boiling water soluble gives the softer finish but is not so easy to use in a classroom situation or if using fragile or not boil-fast threads and fabrics. Unless large scale, remember to pin the work out carefully to prevent shrinkage when first immersed in the boiling water. If the embroidered 'solusheet' is fragile in structure that too can be pinned out on polystyrene when washed away in cold or warm water. Large pieces can usually withstand careful stretching and pinning out to the initial size after the dissolving process.

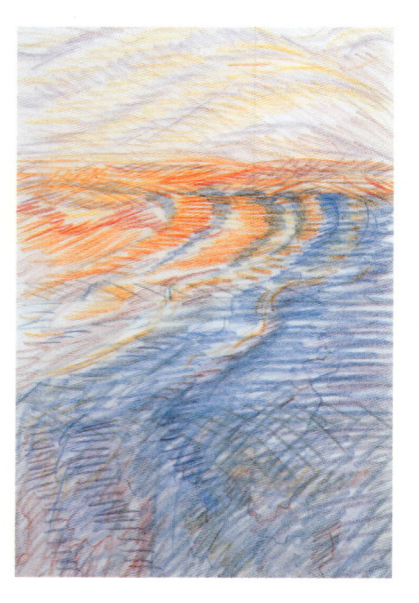

The density and direction of many layers of stitching can distort and shrink the fabric. All of the pieces illustrated lost several centimetres during the work process.

Once 90% of the stitching is complete, wash away the soluble fabric and stretch the damp embroidery on a board, attempting to pin it out to its original size. When dry, trim away or even up any protrubencies around the edges to enable you to reframe the edges of the embroidery with off cuts of soluble cloth so enabling the piece to be placed in a hoop to maintain the tension. Further machining can be worked to decorate, strengthen or refine the edges or any other weak area. Remember to blend both colours and tones within the work so that the piece does not have an obvious edge unless it was planned in the initial design. Wash away the fabric and re-stretch to complete.

- Altering the tone, texture or colour of the bobbin thread can play an important role to blend or integrate various elements. Although not obvious during the work process if stitching on an opaque soluble cloth, the under stitching can be surprisingly effective when the ground cloth is dissolved away. Bobbin colour can underpin a change of top colour helping the blending or merging of the stitching. The bobbin thread plays a supportive role and can add subtle nuances to the work. (see 'Fleeting Moment' page 5)
- Directions of stitch is important even if a matt thread such as Madeira Tanne is used. The play of light on the surface will show a subtle difference.
- The initial mesh or network of underpinning stitches are machined from the centre of the piece and worked outwards. This can help maintain the tension and restrict distortions if that is appropriate for the intended imagery.

**Left Page:**
Painted design showing first ideas for the panel above. Aspects changed during the work process.

The main areas of the design were coloured with aquarelle crayons on 'solusheet' soluble fabric before commencing the stitching.

The fabric set tautly in a hoop frame to machine the straight stitched grid mesh in a toning thread. The next stage is to machine zig-zag stitches haphazardly over the mesh before applying fabrics and working layers of stitch always ensuring that all areas are connected.

**This Page:**
'Into the Sun' - (47cms x 77cms). Inspired by the ridges and hollows observed at Uluru (Ayers Rock). This design became a landscape within a landscape. The aim was to entice the viewer into the distance. (detail)

**This Page:**
Detail of 'Edge of Shade' exploiting the unexpected rich palette of colours observed within the surface of a rock face.

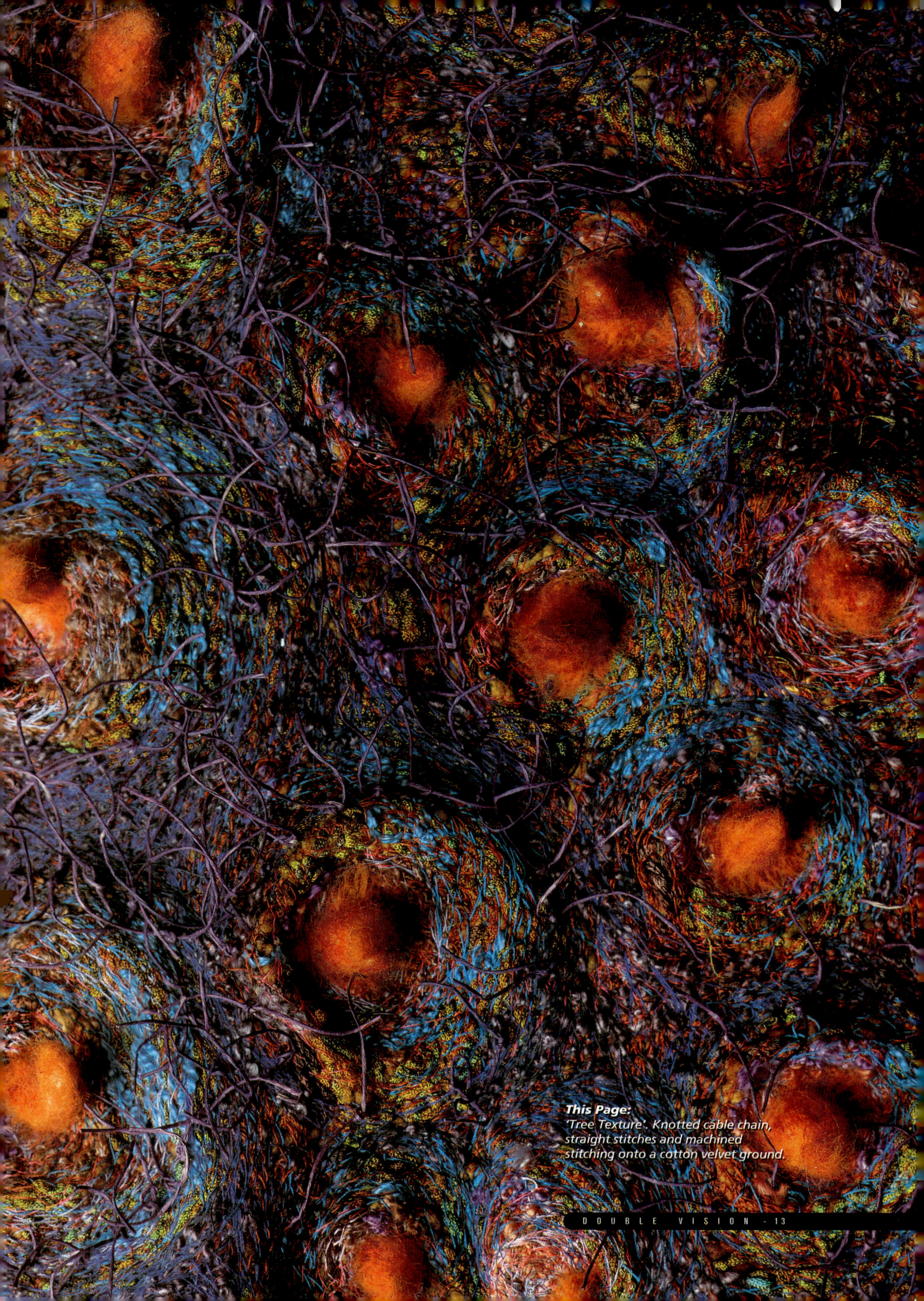

**This Page:**
'Tree Texture'. Knotted cable chain, straight stitches and machined stitching onto a cotton velvet ground.

# Introduction - Jean's Approach

If asked what gives me most professional pleasure then working in my own time and space on ideas that really excite me is invariably the answer.

That is not to say that I don't enjoy the other aspects. The teaching and writing are both enjoyable and require innovative responses to challenges.

Keeping all the elements in balance is a permanent struggle but occasionally an opportunity offers itself and in this case the option of a duo show with my friend and colleague Jan.

To have the challenge of working on an extended body of work was a marvellous chance to really think in depth and develop ideas through to a conclusion.

There was of course the lingering thought that at the end of it I might not have achieved what I set out to do in my own view as well as the view of others.

### Starting

Starting is always difficult and frequently the motivating force is a professional deadline.

Occasionally the challenges are themed and so the subject matter has been selected and these are often the most difficult.

Usually the ideas are self generated and stem from a genuine desire or curiosity to express an idea that has been inspired by an experience or subject.

Although I wanted to begin a new body of work there are elements from the past that continue to inspire and re-emerge in altered guises.

Over many years I have been fascinated by organic surfaces and cycles of growth and decay. The visible scars and marks of the passing of time etched into the landscape and all living things echo human insignificance in the face of natural forces.

Man's effect on the environment and the implied historical references will always inform my work.

Textiles have given me amazing opportunities for travel to places I might not have seen and notebooks or visual diaries are my most important resource. They offer me the opportunity to look more closely and reflect on aspects of other cultures and environments. There is usually some anecdotal reference in most work I do.

So there is rarely a time when I say I am going to start today because any new way of working is a gradual process of refining, selecting and reorganising information that may have been floating about as abstract ideas for some time.

I never underestimate thinking time and the need for thought and reflection.

Naturally there is displacement activity so there are strategies I have developed over the years to help take that first step.

I work with notice boards and before embarking on any new work I remove everything that is not essential and start again by gathering all the aspects of the proposed work that really interests or excites me.

These include drawings, photographs, fabric and thread samples, cuttings, natural forms and any other visual trigger.

Making a careful selection is very useful in identifying the most important elements. This is updated constantly and helps keep me on track when trying to capture the spirit of a piece.

Sometimes I am really surprised by my selection and take time to analyse what it is that drew me to them.

At this stage I have very little idea of the size or form of the proposed work unless a size has been specified by a particular brief.

The evolution of the work will dictate the dimensions and form of presentation.

**Above:**
Notice board - see text.

**Left:**
Detail from notebook -
mixed media with incised wax.

**Far Left:**
Palm fibre collected in Tunisia.

# Visual Diaries/Notebooks

I refer to my visual diaries all the time as they bridge the gap between observation and ideas.

I usually start with observations and these are followed by further drawings where sections of the source may be taken out of context and worked in appropriate mixed media. The process of working through the ideas and reflecting, exaggerating and refining takes over.

I find this totally absorbing and initially only have scant ideas of possible outcomes. The aim is to allow the ideas to emerge as a natural consequence of the design process and not to be too controlling.

It is reassuring to know that when finding new work difficult, time spent developing notebooks always generates ideas. This process cannot be by-passed as it is an excellent way of seeing the source of inspiration with fresh eyes.

Ideas emerge and not all of them will work and one of the real problems is that the more you work the more ideas you get and there is a temptation to work over too broad an area. Having recorded the idea it does take some of the pressure off. Over time the more worthwhile ideas remain exciting and a period of reflection before starting on major pieces is often desirable.

It is usually necessary to work a scale design however briefly just to establish proportions, composition and colour. This is not always detailed as I prefer not to overwork the subject in paper before working with textiles.

# Working in Fabric & Thread

Working with the richness of palette offered by mixed media fabric and thread also has its disadvantages.

There are so many avenues from which to select that it is essential to constantly refer to the source of inspiration and the ideas.

I use only techniques and materials that reinforce the ideas and promote the thrust of the work. The fabrics could range from delicate and fragile gauzes to rich and voluptuous velvets. It is the nature of the subject that dictates the materials

People will prefer some types of work more than others and often say so but you have to go with your own instincts and whatever the outcome you will have developed an idea through to a genuine conclusion.

When discussing personal likes and dislikes with students I try to encourage an objective view of work and the sense that, even though it may not appeal, it is possible to have respect for the integrity of the thought processes underpinning the work.

**Left:**
*Notebook pages exploring organic surfaces using mixed media and paper manipulation.*

**Right:**
*Palm studies 1 & 2 (40cms x 23cms). Mixed media on felt and waxed paper ground with paper fibre and shell additions. (details)*

DOUBLE VISION - 17

# Beginnings...
# Forbidden Fruit 1

**The story of a piece of work.**

During a visit to the USA I saw some traditional Japanese silk embroidery expertly worked.

It required careful handling and was painstakingly stored between stitching to prevent damage. Worked over five years it will be preserved in an archival frame when complete.

Silk is a tactile thread and one that I had rarely used. I became fascinated by the contradiction of using a fibre that is enticing but should be kept beyond reach to preserve it. I also heard a remark to the effect that embroiderers are far too attached to their precious palette of silks and fabrics.

It was almost as if silk was becoming a 'forbidden fruit'.

On the same visit I was lucky enough to see my first real desert around Phoenix in Arizona.

Cacti had never before appealed to me but these huge sculptural forms were very impressive and dominated the arid landscape. They are pillars of moisture and succulence in a parched land and heavily protected by fearsome spines.

They are 'forbidden fruit' and forbidding to all but those adapted to extract the life saving moisture they contain.

A heart shaped prickly pear was the visual trigger that enabled me to combine these ideas.

I was determined to use silk threads to reinforce the idea of the 'forbidden fruit' and combine it with the colours and textures of the Arizona desert. The wire spines contrasting with seductive silk contours were designed to attract and repel the viewer.

There followed further pieces exploiting this idea. Little drops of life giving moisture trapped on lethal spines guarding succulent pillars.

These pieces were worked together and there is no doubt that it is difficult to maintain the momentum if there are too many long interruptions.

**Above:**
'Forbidding Fruit 1' (30cms x30cms). Padded machine over hand stitch ground with wire additions.

## And one thing leads to another...

A trip to New Zealand took the story in a different direction but with the same theme in mind.

Spring in the Northern Hemisphere is New Zealand's Autumn and I arrived in March to find fantastic fruit everywhere, particularly apples.

Apples were of course the original 'forbidden fruit' and the idea of exploring the myth and symbolism of the apple became very compelling.

The apple is a delicious and much loved fruit and yet it has become symbolic of evil and corruption.

The apple in the 'Garden of Eden' was just the start of some interesting research that included biting into lots of different apples and drawing them from all angles. In myths and legends from various cultures there are poisoned apples or the golden apples designed to lure the unwary with their seductive appearance.

A small series of work exploring this theme developed still using a mixture of hand stitching with tactile silk threads combined with machine stitching and culminated in a piece exploring a notion of the apple as a symbol and entitled 'of myth and legend'.

**Top Centre:**
'Forbidding Fruit 3' (31cms x 28cms). Manipulated machine over hand stitch ground with wire and bead additions.

**Top Right:**
'Forbidden Fruit 1 & 2' (each piece 50cms x50cms). Hand stitched linen backgrounds with stitched mixed media central panels incorporating canvas, velvet and machine over hand stitch.

**Lower Right:**
'of myth and legend' (60cms x 40cms). Hand stitch on linen ground with applied machine over hand stitch apples. This piece explores aspects of collection and display.

DOUBLE VISION - 19

# Surface Tension

Successive trips to hot places have highlighted the diversity and rhythms of growing things.

The spectacular patterns and configurations in nature range from the sublime to the bizarre.

Leading on from the 'forbidden fruit' series the ways in which plants grow, reproduce and protect themselves became another compelling passion.

This is particularly evident in palms that not only display incredible visual attributes but also act as a conduit to the past.

The passing of time is evident in the cycles of growth decay and die-back.

Looking at a tall palm against a night sky it is perfectly possible to see why they were so revered by our ancient ancestors. They grow in inhospitable places where little else flourishes and have provided the means of food and shelter for many centuries.

Another of my ongoing interests is the origins of fibre and fabric and the ingenuity of ancient civilisations when adapting whatever they had in their environment to their needs.

Sitting on a beach under a palm umbrella I noticed the ways in which the palms had been used to build fences against the wind and to construct fishing pens in the shallow water and all using traditional methods of tying and knotting.

They can be knotted and woven with the greatest delicacy and made into platters and containers of exquisite craftsmanship.

Over a period of time I noticed that the palm was a recurring image in my notebooks culminating in a trip to San Diego.

I spent some time in a botanical area full of the most amazing palms and other trees. These exotic totems formed the basis of the next phase of my work.

The evidence of growth patterns is there in astonishingly diverse scarring.

Huge oval welts looking like 'eyes' alternate with bands of varying colours.

Jagged tooth like structures protrude in tapered ranks along the length of the upper trunk.

Some have conical thorns similar to rose thorns but much larger.

The fibrous core spills out from fissures and cracks in diagonal patterns revealing the inner structure.

It would seem that the more inhospitable the environment the more aggressive the nature of the plant.

I started with words such as fissures and fans, folding and unfolding, protrusions and indentations, tears and gashes, rhythms and repeats and started to compile an assemblage of the images and ideas that most appealed.

The working title of surface tension seemed to represent the concept I was working on. Sometimes a title helps to keep the focus going.

Ideas for long totem like pillars began to emerge and that was where it started.

**Right:**
*'Surface Tension 1, 2, 3 & 4'
(each piece approximately
36cms x 25cms).
Mixed media grounds with hand over machine stitch with wired and paper extensions.*

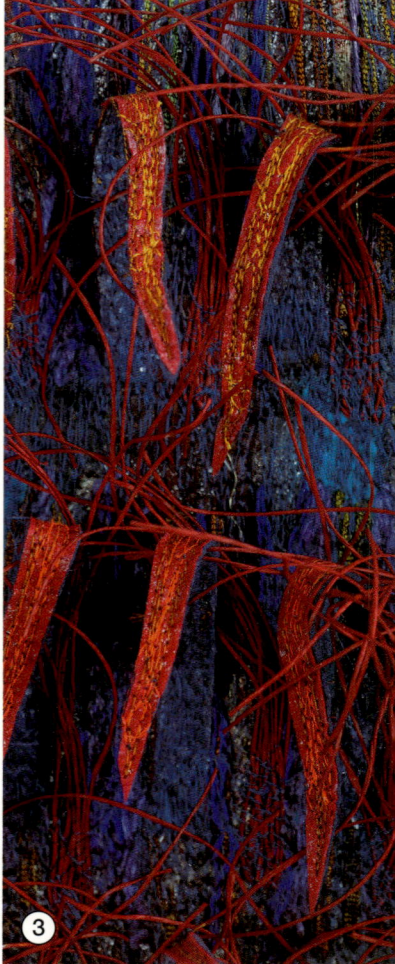

DOUBLE VISION · 21

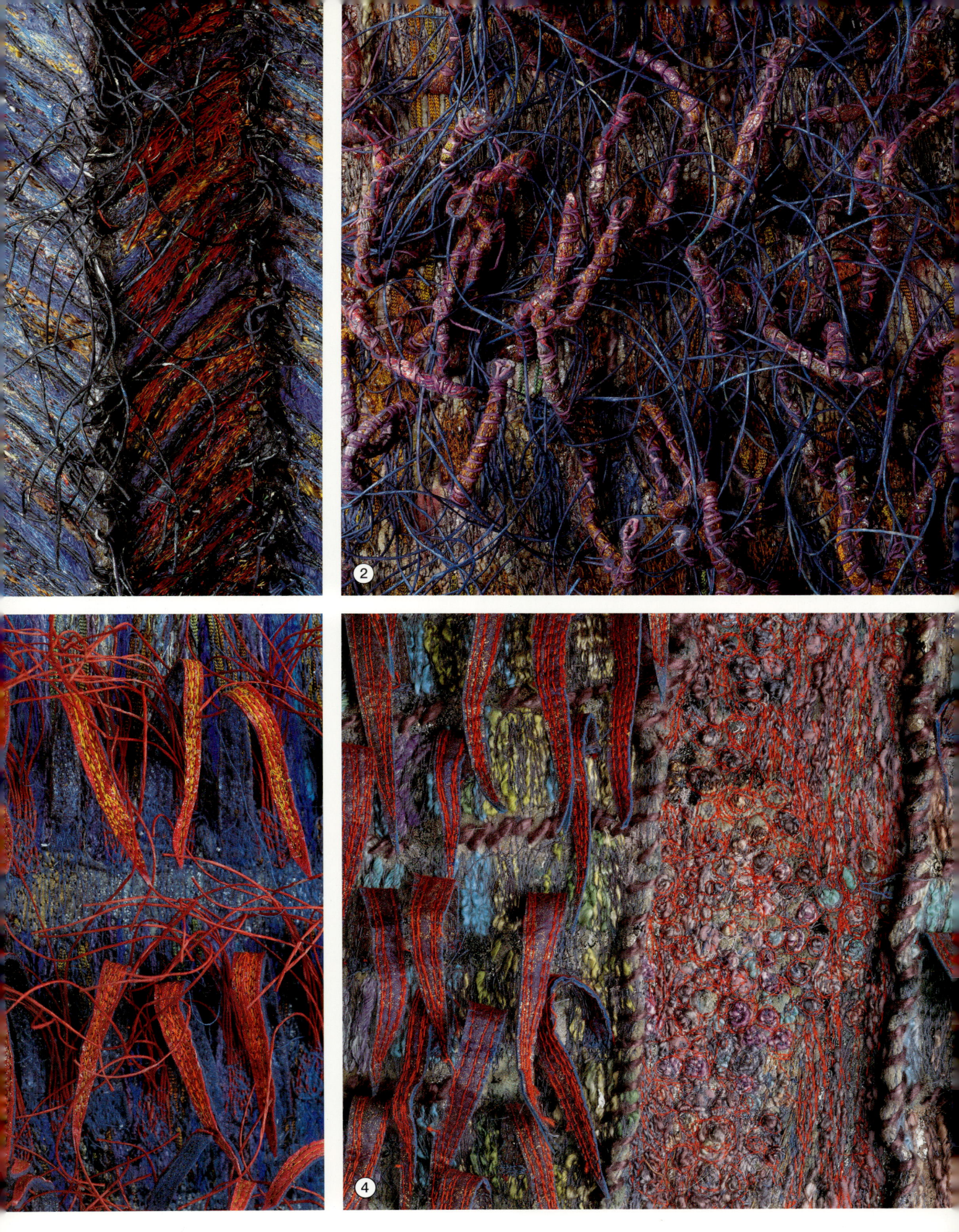

Each piece in this series started by combining words and images and assembling a group of individual pieces that could be viewed as companion pieces and relate to each other or taken individually.

Over a period of time they were started then put to one side to be looked at later and re-evaluated.

This is a luxury as so often a deadline needs to be met and when you see the work later you wish you had more time to make adjustments.

Seeing a body of work grow and trying to view it with fresh eyes is always a challenge.

I fall back on the tried and tested strategies of holding work up to a mirror to see it afresh and of course photographs reveal things not always detected when viewing a familiar image.

It was during one of these review periods that I manipulated the work in my hands and decided that they would work as cylindrical forms simply tied with fibre to hold their shape.

As far as working processes go these may be adapted as the work progresses. Sometimes things work well and at other times you know what you wish to achieve but find it difficult to work out how and with this body of work the protrusions have been a major problem throughout.

I wanted them to grow out of the fabric and to be flexible enough to be rearranged and there were exhaustive experiments to get it right.

The conical thorns were about to defeat me when I met a former student and as we talked I realised she could show me how to 'dry felt' the shapes and this is where serendipity comes in to play. They proved to be the solution and added the extra element I was seeking.

As the deadline approached I felt I had the basis of an exhibition but I wanted to be in a position to select out. The last part of the working process becomes a frenzied flurry of developing remaining ideas and as always there is never enough time to do everything you want.

The fact that you even attempt this is a triumph of hope over expectation.

**Far Left:**
'Totem 1'
(approximately 150cms long).
Cotton velvet ground with hand over machine and felted additions.

**Left:**
'Totem 2'
(approximately 95cms long).
Velvet and felt ground with paper fibre and felted additions.

**Right:**
'Tree of Life 1,2 & 3'
(each piece approximately 75cms - 80cms long).
Machine over hand stitch with paper fibre and other additions on mixed media grounds.

DOUBLE VISION · 23

# The Exhibition

Anyone involved in a major exhibition knows that you cannot keep working to the last moment as there are numerous practical considerations to bear in mind.

The work needs to be securely packed and the padded bags always take a lot longer to make than you plan for.

Elastic bands made with the elastic that can be bought in haberdashers are far easier to pack and unpack than sticky tapes.

Everything needs to be carefully labelled and untitled work given titles or at least numbered.

Photography, if slides or images are needed have to be taken well in advance.

Jan and I have both put up so many exhibitions now that we do not underestimate just how long it takes. Apart from unpacking the work and placing it so that it relates well to the space and each piece is given the consideration and placing it requires, there are many practical aspects that need to be thought out well in advance.

A good tool kit can be built up over years and kept together. Everything should be labelled as things go missing.

Apart from hammers, nails, pins, scissors, screws, bradawl and screwdrivers, a spirit level is essential. Fishing twine is always useful if not to hang then to secure items discreetly.

Staple guns and sticky 'Velcro' pads are very useful. A tape measure or steel rule is invariably needed.

How things are to be hung will depend greatly on the surface. Exhibition boards vary so it is wise to find out beforehand to prevent frustration.

Small safe step ladders are always at a premium.

It is safe to assume that it will take twice as long as you anticipate and to factor in the time.

It is often sad to finish a body of work because you know that it will probably be some time before you have the opportunity to start again but a break is necessary to allow more thinking time for evaluation and new beginnings.

Hopefully the work will have represented the spirit of the subject matter.

It is unlikely that it will all equally successful, but at least with a body of work you have the opportunity to make a committed statement.